PALILALIA

The Hugh MacLennan Poetry Series

Editors: Kerry McSweeney and Joan Harcourt
Selection Committee: Mark Abley, Donald H. Akenson,
Philip Cercone, and Allan Hepburn

TITLES IN THE SERIES

Palilalia

JEFFERY DONALDSON

McGill-Queen's University Press
Montreal & Kingston • London • Ithaca

© McGill-Queen's University Press 2008
ISBN 978-0-7735-3383-7

Legal deposit second quarter 2008
Bibliothèque nationale du Québec

Printed in Canada on acid-free paper.

McGill-Queen's University Press acknowledges the
support of the Canada Council for the Arts for our
publishing program. We also acknowledge the financial
support of the Government of Canada through the Book
Publishing Industry Development Program (BPIDP)
for our publishing activities.

Library and Archives Canada Cataloguing in Publication

Donaldson, Jeffery, 1960–
    Palilalia / Jeffery Donaldson.

    Poems.
    ISBN 978-0-7735-3383-7

    I. Title.

    PS8557.O527P34 2008   C811'.54   C2007-907483-9

This book was typeset by Interscript in 10/13 Baskerville.

CONTENTS

PART ONE

ULTRA SOUND

Spirit whose coming was foretold to us,
why can we not make you out, in the round
bellying wave of the technician's wand,

tumbling there among the iridescent stars
of the cold monitor. Your swimming rings
eddy and swirl like a beamed-down forecast,

from what white-smocked angelic messenger,
of the days to come. Darkness moves
over the face in your mother's waters.

She is blessed among the women who wait
on the darker side of gurney and drape.
Her time is coming. She looks toward you,

not with grace, but the shy, doubtful matriarch's
"who me?" The look we put on, expectant,
bemused, ahead of knowing what we see.

The technician's paddle like a fountain pen
slides effortlessly on the opaque blue
lubricant in a sweeping cursive.

It is shaped to fit her glove like a hand,
but broader, curved slightly at the tip
like a furled tongue, or the lobe of an ear.

Muttering, listening, work-a-day,
she glides her wand over your plump clay,
plies a sculpting thumb to fashion you

from dirt, or deeper into ... what will we
call it in the early years, Play Doh's Cave?
to cast a shadow of who's really there.

You come in such a questionable shape,
we find ourselves half looking for you,
and half for how to see you as you are.

We mistake arms for the man, misread
knee-jerks for too little backbone, and think
that the heart inside you is a head.

You are the boyish throw of arms and legs
in puppetry, footloose Pinochio
lurching unstrung under the footlights ...

You are the drifting astronaut's ghostly face
behind glass dome reflections, lost in space
but for the mother ship's tethering umbilicus.

Infant extraterrestrial, image pressed
to the see-through dark glass, and now – do we
have it clear? – eye to eye meeting our gaze.

"This is the head." The technician points blankly
to another part of the screen entirely.
Your cheeky face vanishes in the murk.

4

She knows her craft. She is past illusion.
She has learned all that gets to you is sound,
echoed sound all that rings back.

She lays her pen down, measures out a line
and takes a pulse, notes any obvious stress,
counts the number of feet. The screen goes black

and the green embers flicker and go out,
like eyelids closed on bright sun that catch
backwashed dissolving palimpsests of light.

A poet long dead, on the life to come,
could hear underground streams murmuring.
I'm content with that, trust that you can hear

the rush of that pulse in your fetal ear,
as we, the assuring hum of a lab
technician's mechanical instrument.

Our deepest soundings are in clear sight,
and they will draw you near,
until the hour we see you face to face,

when out of our senses for the life of us
we call to you by name or laugh for joy,
and not to make light of it, you waul and cry.

BLOCKS

A year now and not a word. Save for baby talk,
dribbled jabber and coo of the infant
now long since part of me. His too many words

scrambled together in the spittled
babble he'll soon part consonant by vowel
into beach chatter or a quiet evening lap talk.

My heart goes out to him, having of late
unlearned how to discriminate
inarticulate sounds from an apt word.

Let's play instead. One evening, dinner done,
toy blocks are spread out for our brief respite.
Miller, set down among them to find his way

out of a labyrinth, questioningly
tries his hand at the scattered alphabet,
etched on palm-sized, cut wooden cubes

spilled over the carpet. Dice to charm
a novice gambler and word-spinner.
He puts one by another and makes a face,

miffed it would seem for lack of what to throw
the devil's bones down into, and read them by.
He monkeys to his feet, staggers out, returns

sidewalling from under the kitchen sink
with a pocked tin basin, and sets to the work
now dimly recognized of casting his lot.

The pictures before him are a mystery.
An *e*, almost always silent in the end,
opens its brief tail at last with a crisp line.

A propped *v*'s precarious vial
looks full only by seeming inclined,
at the least glance, to pour itself out.

An *o*, whose sum of all things lost would prove
oracular, but that the art of being
counted nothing, where it falls, it cannot lose.

And last, a slighted, unassuming *l*,
like an upright man, patient lies down
where all the letters start, and bides its time.

He puts one in and takes it out, a game
with no stakes until he learns to read,
the shapes still puzzling, unput-together.

But now starts to fuss. Nightlong under the spell
of the word he stirs, letter by sole letter,
tippy with sleep, the hour come round at last,

perhaps he hears it whispered at his ear,
perhaps from somewhere behind him or above
feels embraced, raised up, and then finds, like me,

that the blocks have vanished unaccountably,
left in the battered tin mixing bowl thrown
like a sounding brass into the cupboard.

FIRST DREAM

A shoreline, dawnlight, pale mystic weather,
the lake bottom a muddied ochre crust,
the water thinly lapping. A farfetched wooden boat
scarcely big enough for one. Myself, my father,
all hands on the oarless gunnel for the push out.

A caught breath. A boot lodges in the mud.
The hold on the pitching gunnel broken loose.
The hobbled boat staggering in the lurch
with the one, shut-eyed, I can still see clear
into the sepia water out of reach.

My taste for tart grief and for bitter rifts
has not – as the Buddha said it should – let go.
Time I get a grip, see how, for my sake,
the dream set them adrift, a hobbled boat,
a lost one, and a water's give and take.

GLOUCESTER'S DOVER

Among us there is nowhere
From which one could throw oneself down …

W.S. Merwin

I

By the time my father turned seventy-five,
the fluid that for two years sluiced quietly
into his head left his body swimming:

no balance, and a half-foot shuffle
that slowed him to a crawl, without the walker
he refused each time. He'd left behind him

the railroad lamp's arm-swung high-ball
thrown from the box car's side-ladder,
and the nimble leap between couplings.

Despair deepened in his not seeing
any farther ahead now than the lunch table,
and the time it would take him to get there.

His two falls in the bathroom were hard,
feet splayed from under his seventeen stone,
bruises and a gash above his watered eye.

I heard it took two grunting paramedics
and some tub leverage to haul him upright.
Would that he could lean back on his Lazy Boy,

and find himself transported out of sight
to the distant prospect of his last day
without ever needing to climb there.

Now it falls my way to make this unlooked-for
cameo appearance in a supporting role,
the missed, all-but-inconsiderate son

who turns up last minute on Father's Day,
out of the blue: dad's dreamy, always swamped,
scattered and forgetful out-of-towner,

who can never think to pick up a phone,
just in time to catch him inching by cane
into the local Boston Pizza outlet

for a festive steak with the others,
(sisters and mother), now long resigned
to playing out the game short a man.

He double takes at this apparition
so unlike his son, and way ahead of me,
feigns not recognizing the stranger or his voice.

And I too am a little giddy at turning up
out of the middle of nowhere, wide-eyed
at my audacity and lucky timing.

He gives the host our name and takes in stride
the news of a thirty minute wait,
bangs the waiting bench with his cane, and sits.

II

The thing is, about Gloucester at Dover,
(or what the blind man thinks is Dover),
it is the son who stands at a brink,

that wandering there with his lost father,
(whose bloody bandage sponges at lost eyes)
spank in the middle of a flat meadow,

with the sea and Dover's blunt chalky drop
nowhere in sight, Edgar must in fact help
his father to a wish, and make it his own.

Gloucester, he knows, wants to get clear of things,
and one way or another he must play the guide,
help him make the arduous climb up steep

imaginings to an edge, to a limit in himself
that he can't see is there, clear as this
stranger's unfelt, loving face in front of him.

All Edgar knows is this. As matters stand,
arm in arm, father and son can go no farther
than beggar and blind man reasonably might,

and that the father, who needs new thoughts
and will fall badly if he doesn't find them,
must say his farewells alone, drop to his knees,

and finally choose, he imagines,
his own way down into the roaring depths
that he can almost hear, almost see.

He falls to what inside him had seemed distant,
diminished, scarcely a crumb of itself.
To find what, humility and acceptance?

Or in pulling himself upright again
on the arm of a now once more altered son,
accepted signs of a resurrected life.

For all this Edgar fabricates his ruse,
girded in nothing but his small made theatre's
imagined proscenium and its verge.

They scuffle along the unsteep meadow
to verbal heights, whose headlong views in truth
few men ever reach, had Gloucester known.

III

The restaurant hostess calls me back.
I take my father's arm and we start off
inching towards our table of field greens,

water and white bread, that waits, of course,
at the restaurant's farthest end.
We grab menus on the way, and I say

something quiet in his ear of recent days
at home, making it up as we go, how
the garden looked, the car "running good,"

how school was out at last and his grandchildren's
summer days, filled with plans, seemed to stretch out
ahead of them like a wide water without end.

We fix together on his slow shuffle
that drags the time out pleasantly. He knows
the son must leave after the check is paid.

He knows that what contrives the ritual host
at the set table, its budget blandishments,
cannot change him or his fate, and that soon,

when the hour tells, draping his napkin
over the last crumbs, he will rise and shadow
the old steps home. But look how he goes along

with the faux setting and its sheer facade,
and, who fooling whom now, fairly throws himself
into it, as though some final point

had come to him in how he looked at things,
as though an image rose ahead, and the story
about it that he loved, peopled with all

he recognized, was now an easy climb,
and a word was all he needed about …
well, nothing really, to help him make it up.

PALILALIA

for Miller

"Do I hear an echo? Repeating every last word!
I heard you the *first* time loud and clear!
How many times do I need to say it,
your needle's caught in the same groove!"

When Teacher heard you the first time, loud and clear,
at six, trying on each phrase again,
your needle caught in the same groove,
She thought that you repeated things for emphasis.

But six times, trying on each phrase?
Each word beyond reason, extravagant,
even if you did repeat for emphasis.
She could tell you were talking to *yourself,*

in a world beyond reason, extravagant,
like trying to get the roll of a poem right
(as poets tell it … talking to themselves),
cresting the wave's inside rising downfall.

That trying to get the roll of a poem right
is your inheritance, my Touretter's tics,
pulled by a wave's inside rising downfall,
until the right sound falls there into place.

My inheritance, yours, Touretter's tics,
our unruly tongue-clucks, snorts, and growls,
never getting the right sound quite in place,
the obsessive's curse. Revise! Revise

those unruly tongue-clucks, snorts, and growls.
The unfinished poem you circle towards
is the obsessive's curse: revise, revise
always until the listening stills. Let your mind rest.

You *are* the unfinished poem you circle towards.
And if the many times you will need to say it
is an unrest you will always mind, still, let me listen
to hear you echo in every last repeated word.

MUSEUM

But one writes only after one has willed to renounce the will,
and the wisest of poets have always insisted that in the long
run all poetry that is worth listening to has been written
by the gods.

– Northrop Frye

Subway, in the middle of my commute,
    I found myself in a dark corner.
The line vanished into the underground
    in two directions, the clack and crow-screech

of steel wheels echoed in recession
    of the just missed five-o-nine
from the tunnel's depths. Museum Station.
    A chilled solitude widened around me

and water-drops pooled in mimicked snips
    between the rails below. The ceiling lamps'
subdued fluorescence seemed to cast no shadows
    and were like peering through green water.

Exhibits from the ROM in glass cases
    with aboriginal wooden masks descended
like messengers from the real world above,
    whose outsize faces gestured witness and alarm

in the apocalyptic style of indigenous myth.
   Farther up, the February dusk
was tawny, the air tasteless and dull
   as pewter plate. Fog had moved in on

Old Vic's scrubbed-stone but now vague
   turrets uncobbling upwards to the last
vanished spire, as though parting illusion
   from the epigraph above the stairway arch,

still insisting, after these twenty years,
   that the truth would set me free.
All gone up in a mist now, as far
   as I could see. I pictured them above,

the Burwash quad, Pratt, and residence,
   whose faux-gothic walls hold the city at Bay
like the brim of an empty cup, and where
   the mind-set of college years, memories

of what unwritten words, burn perpetually
   as in a crucible. I wonder now had I known,
those years hiding my fidgets, of the tics
   Touretters spend their days trying to release,

or heard of how the obsessive's repetitions
   grind every last impulse to its death
would I have finished more, managed
   the regimental *habitus* and got things done?

Too skittish by far to do as that passage
    from Faust always roared mockingly I should,
from its perch on the cork board above my desk,
    Settle your studies! and sound the depths

of that thou wilt profess. Get real! I still
    have the welts from the nightly tongue-lashing.
But now school's out at last, and the long ghostly
    hours of doodling, daydreams, lectures, lessen.

The students pouring from Northrop Frye Hall
    slushed in out of the fog in private directions
escalating down into the commuter scrimmage
    towards the platform. And that brought it on.

The clapping heal, nasal-snort, the lurching nod,
    the whooped-up screech and cluck.
I tried to catch the right patterns up,
    send them unfolding in dervish rhythms,

unstoppable as blinking. Suddenly,
    out of the unasked-for corporal hootenanny
I sensed a conjured presence whirled out
    in tangents from myself echoing

in the sniggers I bounced off the walls,
    until in my thinking, it appeared,
a stooped man stood apart,
    behind a pillar, unhurried, thoughtful,

neither leaving nor arriving, one I seemed
    to recognize or remember, coming through
and breaking up like a cell-phone signal
    too far from its source. The chunky glasses

and electric hair, plain, perennially ancient,
    he was there, bunched up within himself
like New Brunswick brushwood, swaying
    like a scraggly jack-pine or as a man

in thought at arm's length from a lectern
    will rock, it seems, to captivating rhythms
for the sake of argument. Sheet folder.
    Waiting for this line to take him home.

He spoke up under my own chirps and wheens
    snickering back under the stone work,
like a cold draft working itself out.
    "Still conjuring ghosts, are you Hamlet,

from the depths of the waiting place?
    Have you forgotten my Shakespeare lecture
in '81, on how the Danish spook
    is not one jot less real than the made world

he rises in?" He looked himself over.
    "Not that I can say much in the matter,
but you might have made me younger.
    When you conjure someone in a dream,

(where *are* your manners?) it's best to be more
   generous than time was ... But look at *you*.
Why you look as though you see a burning
   bush or a hanging disk of fire."

"Oh no no, I see you, heavenly ghost,
   old sky father, old officer of art!
but holy company of angels
   what are you *doing* here? Fifteen years

have passed since we sat through the Blake
   readings at your remembrance service,
and together cracked what wine bottles afterwards
   launched you on your way across the Styx,

that second journey you once wrote about
   as having much less to do with ego
than the first. You always looked for how
   to get past it without actually dying,

and I thought if I kept reading your prose
   you might show the way chosen ones take
to the spiritualized secular,
   and find you again, or myself at least.

But not haunting some in-transit concourse
   buried under old grounds I've already trod."
"You're still looking in all the wrong places.
   Time you saw through your own smoke and mirrors."

"A window then? Not a thing I see?"
   "Closer, yes, but don't get your hopes up
on clarity, too many hands and noses
   have been pressed to the glass for you to find

what you're looking for in someone like me,
   even in this state. I was never much
for small talk, as little on subway platforms
   as on that elevator we once rode together."

He shied away three steps and started to fade,
   searched himself as for the rumpled coat
he was still wearing. But I wanted more,
   moved to step clear of my own withholdings.

"I've long imagined I had missed my chance,
   had lost you to the ranks of bygone
paternal mentors, fathers in whom I planted
   the seeds of long-nursed dependencies

for the tall harvest that never came."
   "Still stripping grafts from confidences
greater than your own? You've a way to go,
   and it won't be this old crow, cocking

his eye at you under these shady lights,
   who will get you there. Don't you know
that mine too was the ventriloquist's thrown voice,
   and that what I spoke was a stirred echo?"

"I'll never write as much as you did, spirit,
    the endless notebook-drafts of plumbed inklings
and the thirty odd volumes of limpid prose.
    I can't pinch off a dozen lines in a year."

"You could use some metaphoric roughage
    in your diet. An evacuation and purge,
as Auden said, can be a positive omen.
    But you're the one who goes on about Whitman ...

You have to keep the tics down in public,
    and the vocal dirt from passing at all times,
(like kegel exercises for the mental sphincter ...).
    I can understand that. But your verbal

warm-ups are over-worked, if I may say so,
    too handled and pushed, too proudly shaped.
You'd rather lay off the inkpot than risk
    the odd bad sheet. You won't commit a line

not already hammered into its promise.
    You've got this chiselled-phrase stuff backwards.
A poet *finishes* with cut gems
    for the jeweller's eye, his sturdy maxim's

sculpted waterfall hefted upwards
    into empyrean, he doesn't start there.
You're a Touretter. Why not write like one?
    Hold off the perfectionist blocking out phrases

to exhaustion, those worrying threads,
    the Penelopian back-ravellings of the unmade.
Your repetitious tics have always come first,
    and so they should, the ecstatic rhapsodist's

St. Vitus Dance, slangster's whizzle
    and conjuration, philologist's hullaballoo."
You think of Moses breasting the mountain top
    to find the right words *already* carved

in stone. But Moses too went round and round,
    'til he found the clearing and the words came."
My tics slowed, and he dimmed like a science fair
    light bulb, whose frail filament is

kept lit by the frantic, pumping cyclist
    'til he tires. I cried, "But wait! What words?
Suppose I *do* dance circles, make off-beat
    tongue-claves my first exuberance, tell me

what I'll find there *beyond*." "No time," he said,
    turning away, "and we've both said enough.
But look, you've waited on this line for some time,
    haven't you. I think I hear what you need coming,"

and fading, he said something else I missed,
    when a shriek, as from depths within, drowned him out.
And it was then I saw – what else? – a light
    at the end of the tunnel, and heard the train's

sliced-steel, involuntary skreak and howl,
  an offense to all, but look with how many
along for the ride! One last tic, I sounded
  my barbaric yawp. And a door opened.

THE SHAMBLES: A HOUSE

for Maqbool Aziz, 1935–2000

"I'm so sorry," you quipped for the turned-out
sample-armed Avon seller on the step,
"but Mrs. Shambles is quite beyond your care."

And she, eyeing sceptically the weathered
name plate by the door, "May I speak with her myself …?"
One of the many stories you liked to tell,

this one about the names we give to houses
and what becomes of them. Cycling past yours
each morning on my way to class,

I thought of you inside, unlived with,
stylish and secretive as Jamesian prose,
judgmental, generous to a fault,

detached and circumspect, not withdrawn.
We locked horns over Virginia Woolf,
left loudly from your British reading list

("let me tell you this … no, no, she is *very* bad"),
your inexplicable disdain at last made clear
by a friend, only once you'd died, as based

unspokenly on the Jewish question,
yourself utterly silent on boyhood days,
parents or siblings, your roots in Pakistan.

Bucking the lawn-habit of your beloved Westdale,
you kept a garden lavishly in front,
stone pallets, an always early magnolia

dropping its white empty cups in the snow,
to bring with your natural ceremony
the first signs of spring to the neighbourhood.

You'd wake early for morning class, cycle
so slowly down the road, I would joke
about setting my kick-stand not to pass.

You played tapes of the poets, or held forth
in choice anecdotes, brushing in broad strokes
the life you believed was largely unlived,

if ours, evidently, for the choosing.
I felt your headstrong, earnest style made light
of my own quixotic hysteria.

One of the good things about verse … we can turn
back among endings. In one, you might see
an unforgetting colleague's circling past

your door at winter dawn, raising an eye,
teared-up by northerlies, to note the long-sold house
no longer a shambles, new lawn given to seed.

But in the end come around to this final line,
where, retirement but two months hence,
you slyly dodge the departmental send-off

we never get to plan, and show the way,
that night before your heart first felt a squeeze,
by walking out in the midst of a bad play.

GARDEN VARIATION

An Epithalamium for Glen and Elizabeth Gill

All gardens in their season dig like prows,
lift and plunge, fountains of water lunging
on all sides ahead of their fresh breezes.

But there is a moment that the painter loved,
in later August, so the story goes,
at dusk, when blue still backs the gold leaf,

and before the sun's incandescent wick
slips under the rim of the shallow bowl,
when the air is opened like a decanter

and breathes and is poured out over the stone
pools, still warm, and the faery lanterns
that children bring glow like dimmed chandeliers.

And there is an arbour where amorists
might lie down, and without which the garden
would lack its metaphor of the nuptial canopy.

In June, the sunsets are garish, July's
parched ferns nod in the haze, and September's
patchwork regalia always flags in the trees.

No, it was August he came back to those evenings,
for the same twenty minutes, with the case
of paints under his arm, and set to work.

And we may never know how many times,
for that one scene, he returned to finish
what he'd started, what menial tasks detained him

at the house, what single cloud mass sauntering
through his sky at the pace of a hay wagon
lengthened the days between his return visits,

what stretch of unlucky rains intervened
in the given weeks, when he was all but ready,
or indeed how many long winters passed

when the hard ground was jabbed with sticks
and the bitter northerlies made
any trip to the garden a waste of time.

And in the end, to judge by the painting,
it might as easily have been winter
the whole year round, where the painter lived,

and never the best possible moment
to go looking for the unfastened light
full of serendipitous intention.

We really just have the story itself
of *Natura Naturans*, the garden unfolding,
as he called the final landscape that years

after was discovered among his works,
the floating lanterns, the breathing air,
the gold leaf, the lovers' nuptial arbour

and its short-lived gloaming, ephemera he loved
so well he went back to get them right
just for that once, more times than we will know.

VANISHING POINT

To my wife's memory of her mother
Cornelia Abma, 1930–1979

Think of the old keeper, the quiet one,
glimpsed in that ochre-bricked Dutch-master
interior of fore-room and back room.

In her kitchen, in her chair, she is long past
the tied-up drape's satin proscenium
and the airs of the closed garden aside.

Her peace is not a moment but a place,
her hour like a dwelling's roomy puzzlements
gracefully articulated back and back,

far beyond the foreground's theatrical
domestic intrigue. Your restless eye lights
on her there. Peer at her work and the brush

that makes her what she is, at the heart of it,
and grieve the home's original design.
All you needed to reach her was more time.

I love to think of you. Even, I should think, of you
somewhere else now arching your back in love
(in the tight-limbed, unspeakable knot
we have long got around coming to),

while a witty tongue not from my own mouth
goes at your thigh to the soft glottis
even you can't see, or tell, as the tongue moves,
what its next utterance might be.

There now. A syllable flicks you over
one more broken cry not nearly the last.
You fall back. The tongue is withdrawn.
Your lips seal after it and your mouthfolds breathe.

Rapture is your first solitude. I can feel it,
and afterwards think you must feel something
open inside you at a word. My love,
the pleasure, take it from me, is all mine.

PART TWO

WHILE WE GROW TIRED,
LIKE SWIMMERS

When the armed man fires his warning shot
into the air and the recoil crooks his arm
for an instant, does the bullet he fires rise

at 500 metres per second per second
only for a while, until it reaches, say,
a gravid apogee among the clouds, stops,

then lies back like water at the fountain top,
falls, not to land with a clink, but carried sidelong
by winds and lost amidst the snow and rain?

Or does it continue onwards, make light
of the earth's rotation and its gravity,
break from the outer sky and join the eternal

procession of all objects in perpetual motion,
farther unslowingly into the vast
oceans of space, until it kills something?

So many, I thought, never have so many undone
their terricloths and stepped testily
into the flat water. New ones
snowshoe thickly across the burning sand.

The life-guard is beautiful, a wave in his hair.
He sits atop the whitewashed-trellis tower
loftily, seven feet in the air, and stares ahead.
He has designer sunshades, a superior tan.

The flipped-down sign below him says
"CJ Poole, Life-guard," in black and white,
and one in red and white, unseen beneath,
says "Danger, waters unsupervised."

Neither the head nor the torso moves.
There is nowhere he does not see.
He has never lost a soul, nor saved one,
though all about him the living come and go.

Late afternoon. Snow. Far from the house.
In a sky alcove a lightly coaled fire
crumbles and settles, though at its side
clouds piled and ranged like unkindled pine
would keep the land warm as a sitting room
for hours still, were someone tending to it.
But there is no one, far as I can see, who stirs
in that upper room, above the pine wood,
with mind enough to keep a lasting fire
burning past its time. Through unlatticed air,
I can watch the dimmer embers
tinker to ash, and already I think ...

why should it fall to me always, out here
alone, to keep the blessed thing going.
Any one could tell, to see me hesitate,
how the story beneath it, with its downcast
umbrage white-canopied for the long season,
has got too gloomy for me to go into.
And who knows but that the fire within,
itself long cooled to the cramp of lit spaces
and what by this light is clear would be
a dark loft without it, high as wide fields
and starry night air, just wants to go out.

RIDDLE

When a rose begins to die,
it will wilt and drop its petals
　　in no pattern on the table.
Just one of several reasons
　　oblivion is unstable.

LESSON BY CANDLE-LIGHT

Unwasted ash is what we ask
of the candle and the dark line
that runs through it.
But it will come to nothing
if like me it holds
itself the wrong way
under the crescent light
that shines overhead
and what part is
warmly touched
runs soft and cools
into other forms any flame
would go out on.

For the steady candle burns
to become less of itself,
shallowed like a crucible
under the loose gold leaf
that sips from it invisibly,
until it runs out in the end,
is used up, the way whatever
good thinking there was
at the start of this poem is,
this poem that I've always known
would end with the black cone
that pinches dark lines.

PART THREE

EROGENOUS ZONES

For Christina Brooks

CATCH

I stood in a boat once on the water,
half asleep, casting lines at the centre of a lake.
Hours without a strike and all was still.

Patchwork sky, sunfall, flat water
scarcely dimpled by the lure-drop. And then
I turned, and the air changed, and a wind

fumbled the tightened surface into pursed
kisses, or loose-wrapped, overripe plum skins,
darkening purple. The waterlight's

blousy stitches unbuttoned, lengthened wide-wise,
fell open clear through, the chilled circles
inside them shrinking. And then all was swoon

and flummox, stirrings-up, the underswell's
bob and joggle rising and falling.
And there I was, in the middle, part of me

roused by the buoyant frisson stretching itself out,
the other clutching a thin shirt at the neck
against the rude, suddenly stunning cold shower.

I was slow to find my taste for cashews,
a connoisseur of peanuts till drinking age.
But the winking mistress in "Seeds and Grains"

at the local market couldn't believe
I'd never tasted. She reached down and came up
with what she called a fine sample between

thumb and forefinger. I had seen one before,
but not this close, and not with all the time
I had there to finger its shape and size.

It looked like a pinky tip perched gingerly
over a tea cup, or a fiddlehead's first
nubbed bud that folds out from the fern hood.

I thought, "gobble 'er up, it's small." But no,
she showed me cashew patience, how to pinch
it gently in your teeth, take the salt off it

with your tongue in slow circles until
the seam loosened and it came open
in your mouth and you tasted the pungent oils.

Then she told me the price. More dear, she smiled,
because of the nurturing they require, and the hell
we have trying to break them from their shells.

CAVE

The bush was no obstacle. I could crouch
half backwards and fiddle-work my fingers
clear to the thick parts without getting jabbed,

past leaf-veins unlapping fold by fold
to snug partings, to the raised mound beneath it
I was sure no living soul had ever seen.

I was the stout neighbourhood explorer
of nether worlds, gateways to the bowels
of the earth, from whose bourn no child returns.

But I was no child. I swiffed the brush aside,
groped in, and saw ... hell! it wasn't a cave,
but an unmanned mine's unfathomable drop.

And many *had* been here: an iron railing
like a spiral flagpole, and steps that circled
as straight down as would scarcely break a free fall.

I leaned out and dropped hoots down like buckets,
but each call clattered back, tipsy with vertigo.
I was in limbo, and dreamed some pagan spirit

had a hand in this, down past flipper swims
of jelled air and walls that drip wet run-off
into plumb pools at the bottom, where surely

each drop's intermittent ping tapped
at a stillness and spread languorous waves
of infinitesimal purls outward and down

to what depths I would never know, and God
knows never see. It was too dark and deep
to light even its own stirred likeness,

least of all the look of one whose face
would have shone there, shimmering in the midst
of a perfect heaven opening above his head.

RESCUE

The fireman's red fire hat makes him a hero.
It has a long sloping brim that drains hosed
water off his back. It always goes in first,

pulled down snug, for those rare, heated moments
he must leap headlong over loose debris,
through the burning hole and the narrow wall

of a suburban nursery. There is a life at stake.
He keeps one eye open in the smoke,
and dowsing all around him where he prods,

finds what child a woman's lost somewhere inside,
wrapped in a warm swaddling. Helpless,
it grabs the slippery rim as he pulls back,

holds tight all the way out, and then lets go.
The tumult abated, then and only then
can our man tilt the dripping hat brim back,

or better, lay it down beside a now
pulled-off rubber suit crumpled in the bilge,
and smile broadly, with his boots still on.

There were two docks at Uncle Steven's cottage,
a cedar dock almost chubby as I was,
built out over shallow rocks on the porch side,

and a slender one made of flexible,
articulated parts that loped gangly
from the house, perpendicular. It crossed

over the rock shelf and gave a night's mooring
to visiting boaters. I tied my own craft
to the short one, for better launch handling,

but for daydreaming and deep plunges off
the long end, I preferred walking the plank.
I loved how it gave a little when you

put some weight on it, undulant buoyancy
cantilevered on invisible floats,
never at one with its lazy arc and swag

when I went all the way, but in the end
thrilled at how it sprang back up, the instant
I dove free and got my fat load off.

SEED

I once found two grouse eggs in a leaf nest
on the ground at the base of a dried stump.
They were marble coloured and speckled.

It was cool and some of the mountain winds
hung on past the forest ridge to scuffle
the ground cover like crumpled paper.

I looked but the hen was nowhere in sight.
It was neither early morning nor evening,
not the hour to be away from the nest foraging.

They were alone. I wanted to touch them
but thought better of it, instead reached
to cup my hand under the damp leaf mould

and gingerly raised them, palm-jostled, to measure
their weight and contour, feeling for the mass
of slippery brasses rolling with each fondle.

But they were too light to be anything but empty.
I could not put them down gently enough,
Even with nothing jumping to hurt inside.

Robert Frost once wrote about picking apples,
how in mid-day dreams their russet colours
drifted before his eyes like temptations,

like the auguries of a second fall,
whose labours made you want to lie and sleep.
He pulled at each pendant fruit until it gave,

and handled it with gentleness, a care
that people only use with chores they love.
Not like those rude gropes at the first fall,

when Eve and Adam, until then enjoyers
of a sanctioned coitus, decorous
as blown window sheers, found the itchy fruit,

bit hard, and leapt at their first, no – can you
imagine? – the *mother* of all floor wrestles.
"Rough sex" we call it now, with a frisson.

We've been left ever since to pick *and* choose.
I once saw an elderly Chinese couple
on St. Clair, returning from the market,

husband and wife, keeping five grim paces
between them, she behind, according
to some ancient and unspoken custom.

At the husband's thigh knocked a gravid bag
of thin fabric, down to its last threads,
the drip-dry sort that needs to be ironed

but never is. Clearly, he'd used it for years,
lugging various nectars and small fish
until they made it home. What pulled on its sad

wrinkles were two small, dark eggplants,
whose plumb weights cast them mildly
pendulous, bumping his thigh widdershins

on each returning stride. She kept her space.
Their long years had brought them fruits of knowledge,
and a bond that left no doubt who did the chore

on the kitchen table, opened and reached in
for the unbruised gourds, as Frost once said,
to cherish in hand, lift down, and not let fall.

ODE ON A HENRY MOORE

Bold Lover, never, never canst thou kiss ...

I first saw the Henry Moore sculpture
on Dundas Street when I was twelve,
first love Ellen Tanner on my arm,

first kiss surely pending, on our class trip
downtown to the Ontario Art Gallery.
Ten foot donuts as Dali might have cast them,

half-deflated and misshapen O's
slumping like Oz's bad witch to the sidewalk.
Butts were tossed in each hole's bottom lip,

if you could call them lips, Toronto's tasteless
smoke habit sooting the stale air inside.
Innocent forms, they rose to meet half way,

each turned aslant to brace the other's curves,
uncoupled, not yet consummated,
but still poised roundly on their crescent brims

that circled, opened wide, and took you in,
scarcely a breath in the cupped gap between.
We stalked the bronze castings from all sides,

self-styled connoisseurs of some antique urn,
like the ones we moaned sham yawns over
in the galleries. Then climbed up inside.

Ellen squeezed into the one gullet, winked me
towards the other one across and leaned out,
puckering up, eyes closed and waiting.

But when I climbed in I was all tongue-in-cheek,
skittish, mouthing coquetry and dangling
my clapper out the side with mock theatrics.

She rolled her eyes of course and jumped down.
I lost her, what with no one there to say
what I knew on earth and what I'd need to know.

Paul was his name, timid, lover of dares.
One March, he showed me the sewer outlet
that took up Black Creek's thawing effluent,

a cement bunker that backed out sideways
from a hill, with even-spaced narrow steel gratings
barring the hole. He said I was too chicken

to go in alone, or a mama's boy,
or a pansy afraid of getting hurt.
And he was probably right. Eleven,

already I knew what "filth" my father
told me passed through these parts each time we flushed.
Not to mention the disease you could pick up

just for going in. Was it the bragging rights
to say I'd entered forbidden places?
Or was it the one spot in town a boy

my age could hear the underground rush empty
from hearing, its taut rapids purling in the mind
long after, as in the hollows of sea shells.

No matter. The bars made for a tight squeeze,
but I played cocksure and dextrous, unbuttoned
a puff-down winter parka, hitched it up,

and with a few awkward hip turns made it in
on my hands and knees, found myself snug.
What was there left but to screw my courage

to the sticking point and head for the dark?
I twisted round and gave Paul a look that said
it wouldn't hurt if he came in behind.

PART FOUR

And what would it be like
if the mind in afterlife
outlived itself, and dwelled
in a single sound or sight.

And nothing but that thought.
Say, a daughter runs to kiss,
or Mozart coins a phrase,
or a lover flicks a clasp,

or a window spares a breeze,
or bread's washed down with drink,
or a last gold tips the trees.
How nice, you think.

But that their repetition,
more sums than you can tell
of unendable millennia,
would be a kind of hell.

Which is why I think, for me,
like this flower in a jar
(watered to keep awhile) is what
nothing at all would be.

A GLOSS ON
"CROSSING BROOKLYN FERRY"

I am with you, you men and women of a generation,
or ever so many generations hence …

You there who have come at last after our many years,
I know why you stayed apart the way you did,
after we'd made every show of being welcoming and agreeable.
You must have guessed by now that we were waiting for you.

We got dressed each day and cleared our throats.
We laid books open on our knees and read aloud
from them and book-marked the best passages. We made phone calls.
We put out more than enough chairs and then stood back.

We built roads for you to show the way here. They lay in every
direction at once. We bought large pitchers and found things
to pour out from them until you came, sat around your TVs,
arms about each other, and never once looked over our shoulders.

We rushed to the top floors of buildings. We took broad strides
in the fields. We used your sun to grow the vegetables
that you never ate because you never came nearer to the baskets
than you were. We chose our places at the latest supper.

Even love. We met your ancestors and made love to them,
taking care to make lots of noise, but only found ourselves
crowded with more children who stood up and shook their heads no.
Finally we became your dead, laid down for you in the graveyards

like red carpets, and spread ourselves over rivers like confetti.
We were hurt of course that you kept your distance even
when we felt sure it was time. But now you have the chairs
and the tables that were yours from the start, your baskets

filled with vegetables, your pitchers and TVs, even the books
that you can read now for yourselves, and the sun, the sun above all,
and of course you know what we failed to learn in our time here,
that all you had to do was not come when we called.

Are we at last the belated ones?
It is too early to tell.
But the one who sets toast
on a table, or the sad one opening

a sock drawer, or the dark riser
who steps with the morning news
onto the 6:20, unmissed
by the sleeper under flowered covers ...

they are like caretakers
setting chairs out for guests
who have not yet arrived
in the auditorium,

are not yet born who will hear
what is spoken there, when it is,
after the scrape and shuffle,
let alone listen.

TIMED EXPOSURE

Photograph of a nude lit by a field
of snow. In the all-but-empty room,

antique sofa squared at its centre,
she lounges on her stomach,

buttressed on elbows, her breasts
like plumb lines above a pillow,

head lowered, one foot crooked at the knee,
and holds her body something like

perfectly still, in the shivered, ice-white
late evening winter dark.

She steadies her posture of calm.
Snowed in with light,

the ubiquitous blank blaze
snatches her held foot blurred.

Remember, just this once,
that when the bared flesh shines it is

still in the dark, a dark we picture
not there at all, or that wouldn't be,

could we at every instant
hold our eyes open long enough.

Is it the man dead a thousand years – only just this week rising
out of a bog with a befuddled gulp – or the one who passed away
last Tuesday in Sudbury, who knows being dead the best?
Or which is it, the man dead a hundred or a thousand years
who only now begins at last to understand how they have hardly
even started being dead, that they are innocent and naive still
in the breadth and scope of their personal nullity,
their burgeoning irrelevance and compromised ubiety.

Which of them would be free to speak most passionately
of how once we die we don't stop being dead ever,
not even once, not even for a little while.
Does it follow that we must get better at our deaths
after a time, and better still after great amounts of time?
For what more have we to do, even now, but improve
on the depth and current of our present state, whatever
it happens to be, walking to a place, or just sitting about.

I think of the man who hanged himself in our nearby woods
in 1973. His funny purple feet stuck out from under a sheet.
He must have despaired of his personal prospects
and imagined with relief being free of the hard labours.
I never really thought until now of trying to help him
be all he could be among the dead by recalling that he was.
And I have no idea whether he has got better at it
since then or not. Or worse, whether he has given up trying.

Were we wrong to arrive so soon, full of plans and gumption?
Is this neither the time nor the place for us to be

dressing up for one another and paying our compliments?
Have we come far too soon for our helpings of bread and wine?

No one can say. But would we hurry so to our posts if we imagined
how dated those who follow after us will think we are?

Be honest now. Don't you have the feeling, though you might never
say so, that the peasant farmer who stands looking over

his master's crop of grains in the year 1245 and who
even now has his back turned to us was a little naive

or short sighted to have stood up so long ago to be counted,
at a time bound to become the deep past eventually?

Was it impatience that made him leap so early?
Think of his wife, a plain looking woman with four children

who blushes to be told she doesn't look a day over 30
and turns aside to think with quiet relief of how much future

is still left to her (maybe fifteen years). It is centuries
since she last got up to see about breakfast. Look at them there,

he bends to the earth, parts a chafe in his fingers, tests
the wheat for moisture. She must be stomping on the grapes.

The grave marker laid for them when they died is dirt now,
and their names are not written in any of the sad annals.

And what about us? Do we think of those who will live 300 years
from now and who know more about our future than we ever will?

We tried to look better than our ancestors at just being here,
imagined ourselves levitating above the long afternoons

and thought about not falling behind any more, god knows,
than we already had, and really did make an honest effort

to start on the long lists, make headway on the cluttered attic,
and this day above all others take time as it came. That is,

if we hadn't used it up already, the hour long since
spoken for, and set our alarms for first thing the next morning,

when we would surely rise, dress, and bring up that fresh jar
of preserves from the cellar, and this time with our hearts

in it watch at the window for the first sign of those
who now do all their thinking about us for themselves.

What would it be like if we saw everything
in front of us now as a distant memory,
if each present moment – this one, for instance,

where I rise from the breakfast table
and by chance find myself in what looks
to be a scene out of a painting entitled

"A Cup of Coffee Brought From the Kitchen
and Put Down on a Table By the Window
Where it Sits Now in Quite a Lot of Light" –

what would it be like if each present moment
that we lived through were experienced
at the very time as though it were in fact

already the memory we would have of it
thirty years hence, already reduced
and simplified, erased or broken down

into the chimeras that flicker in the mind-fog.
Being here now would take the form
of how you might one day look back at it.

Think of that walk home from school
when you were seven, the crack in the sidewalk,
the question now of whether or not

there were trees because you can't quite see them
anymore, though you have the dim impression
that they were there or must have been.

What would it have been like if the moment
then, the very moment as you lived it,
were exactly as you picture it now,

and the sidewalk you moved along seemed somehow
not there at all and you felt a heartache
at not seeing it any better than you could,

so that the time between two dim images
of your foot falling on the sidewalk
and of your hand on the door of the house

where Mother must have been waiting
for you was a blank even then,
not filled out with the trees, sky, and people

you imagine you've forgotten. And as years passed
nothing had changed but your belief that the walk
must have been more real at the time, though it wasn't.

It would be like lifting down from the top shelf
the old softened puzzle box, too many of whose
1000 pieces that you thought were lost

all these years, leaving the final picture forever
incomplete, in fact came just like this on the day
you first tore off the wrappers and raised the lid.

Or perhaps it isn't as bad as all that.
And maybe our memories are more powerful
than we ever dreamed and we don't know it.

Imagine for instance that the hour at hand
is not really at hand at all, that now
isn't now but thirty years from now,

and that before you are the concrete details
of perfect memory, the present moment
before you – with the cup there and the table

and the light – in all its immediacy
is what you have at last called to mind
after years of practise and concentration.

You could just open your eyes, and say, look,
that cup I broke years ago, here it is,
whole again, and that table I never liked,

so palpable to the touch, and heavens,
those iris-widening shadows I hardly
ever glanced at in the curtained light

are summoned here in my living memory,
and look how well I do it, and how free
it turns out I was to give it all away.

LET

For Richard Outram, in memoriam

God was good with words. He knew it.
He turned a phrase, and said, *Let there be light,*
held it up in the darkness, then threw it
down before our dazzled sight.

Not, "It's time, light! You should start to be!"
or "Stand back folks, I'm gonna make some light!"
But just the right words to set, oh, *nothing* free
at the right time. A calculated *ought.*

He knew the secrets of our wistful "Let,"
The "what would happen if …" subjunctive spell.
Not the *ex nihilo* Erector Set
of scaffolding and girders, where the hell

you fashion from hard iron's bound to break,
for aught made out of naught's illusion still.
But now, say "let …," for mere allowance's sake,
and openings will fill with … what you will.

Flash back to mathematics class in school,
the teacher brooding tall at his blank slate,
like a deity, makes you seem a fool
by writing out long formulas of great

impenetrable equations, undefined,
a Sanskrit algebra of xy pairs
ramified in patterns out of mind,
a sprawling orrery of whirling stars,

that I must somehow solve, when teacher says,
in his English brogue … "Let x equal light"
Did I hear that straight? "Come again, Sir, please,"
and his patience thins, "Let it equal … *eight*!

What is your answer now?" I stare in the abyss.
It escaped me then, the longed-for solving grace,
that the world is nothing but hypothesis,
its great unknowns, the cosmos, time and space,

all algorithms of what might appear
were worlds made out of would-that-it-were-so.
I might have just replied, had I God's ear,
"Better than nothing, Sir, for all I know."

ENTER, PUCK

Up and down, up and down;
I will lead them up and down:
I am fear'd in field and town;
Goblin, lead them up and down.

My cultural horizon was a single line,
   airy, chilled, smoke-coloured ice
three degrees below freezing, the sound
   of clacking sticks like rolled dice,
the hour and the sky always the same.

   Midwinter rinks are their own season,
hard and precise, oval shaped, 200 feet.
   My theatre then was a hockey rink,
a proscenium arch laid horizontal.
   Drama was what you could taste in the air

when the game was tied, just minutes to go,
   and even classical dance no more
than the twirling sashay of our more cocky
   scorers in the neighbourhood. I was fourteen,
had tried poems, but still spent every spared

   minute on the back-lot hose-watered rink
firing pucks at two piled railway ties.
   By high school, there were three books I'd read:
Bower on goal tending, a paperback
   of Leaf stats, and a life of Mr. Hockey,

Gordie Howe. But in grade nine English,
    when I looked up summoned from whatever
make-shift game-board's impromptu power play,
    I could sometimes follow upwards of three
whole sentences Miss Pearl's trying lecture

    on courtly Shakespearean make-believe.
A month of Tuesdays, the class took up
    the bard's dream of a midsummer night,
something about a king's stately pastimes,
    selves lost and found, and a comprehending

canopy of trees outside the court, where magic,
    with the help of aery sprites, brought folks
to their senses. But never mind. The stage
    she conjured – out of court or wood –
was so unlike our winter's tale of slate-grey

    suburban skies, blunt trees in the snow banks
like jabbed-in hockey sticks left-behind,
    and sad sounds like chalk nicks on a blackboard,
I scarcely bothered to listen. Get a life!
    Teacher, as always found me broken loose

on unfettered, imagined breakaways,
    all down-river without a goal in sight.
She looked down with unravelling patience.
    "Welcome back, Mr. Donaldson, so glad
you could join us. Perhaps we could put

those mumblings of yours to better use.
Read for us please from Act II, Scene ii,
   Line 59. Start at 'Enter, Puck.'
Toby, point out to Jeffery where we are."
   I was showed my place and swallowed hard.

"Enter, Puck." I suppressed a rising snort,
   and heard a snicker like it from the back,
and then two more, then general giggles,
   and almost to preempt them I tried once more
"Enter, Puck," more gingerly, uncertain,

   to hide an unselfconscious double-take.
I had dragged my whole dreamworld's assembled
   stage-flats and its band of players into class,
where they lingered on like brief chimeras
   to haunt and foil better purposes.

I was no fool. I knew the prankster Peter Puck,
   the cartoon, talking, two-legged rubber disk,
defier of gravity, whose song and dance
   conjured finer aspects of the game
during breaks on Hockey Night in Canada.

   But that there should be another like him
to do a master's bidding, to cast vexing
   whammies on all the players he touched,
send them scuttling in a tizzy after him,
   seemed to me more than reasonable.

So read, "I go, I go; look how I go;
    Swifter than arrow from the Tartar's bow."
A master himself of harmless outdoor mischief,
    almost benevolent, selfless, single minded,
here was a Puck potent as a talisman.

At last, I thought, a bard who knew what end
of the hockey stick was up. But Shakespeare?
    I didn't know the game went back that far …
But there he was, if no more than a spot,
    pixilated and untrappable,

eluding capture, springing free, tumbling
    and deflecting sportive among the players.
Hobgoblin, you were the black trickster
    that kept me up anights staring at walls,
replaying your shenanigans, your devilish flips,

with each flitting gesture across the dark
expecting always more dextrous miracles.
    It was like reaching to touch the wood frame
of an amulet, what for me in time
    became the sole power of conjuring, in a word,

but for now manifestly real and firm
    as the deft weight of India rubber.
It gave me whatever gumption I had lacked
    to recite my last words aloud with confidence,
and read unknowingly for the first time

the line that would spring me open, years on,
as the scot-free boy, chasing in daydreamed
break-aways, up and down, up and down,
the slipped spirit, the bouncing elusive Puck:
"I am that merry wanderer of the night."

ACKNOWLEDGEMENTS

I would like to acknowledge the generosity and support of the editors of the following journals, in which certain of these poems first appeared, occasionally in earlier versions: *The Antigonish Review, The New Quarterly, The Alabama Review.*